TIME
FOR KIDS

BEHIND THE CANVAS

An Artist's Life

D0832119

Blanca Apodaca
Michael Serwich

Consultants

Timothy Rasinski, Ph.D.
Kent State University

Lori Oczkus
Literacy Consultant

Based on writing from
TIME For Kids. *TIME For Kids* and the *TIME For Kids* logo are registered trademarks of TIME Inc. Used under license.

Publishing Credits

Dona Herweck Rice, *Editor-in-Chief*
Lee Aucoin, *Creative Director*
Jamey Acosta, *Senior Editor*
Heidi Fiedler, *Editor*
Lexa Hoang, *Designer*
Stephanie Reid, *Photo Editor*
Rane Anderson, *Contributing Author*
Rachelle Cracchiolo, *M.S.Ed., Publisher*

Image Credits: cover & pp.1, 4, 16, 22–23, 30–31, 36 (right), 37 (top) Getty Images; pp.5, 7, 8, 9 (middle), p.17 iStockphoto; pp.18–19, 26–27, 32–33 J.J. Rudisill; pp.12 (left), 13, 24, 25 (right), 29, 34 (left), 35 (top) Newscom; p.11 akg-images/Cameraphoto/ Newscom; p.40 (top) akg-images/Newscom; pp.12–13 Splash News/Newscom; p.23 (bottom) The Granger Collection; p.25 (left) Édouard Manet [Public domain] via Wikimedia Commons; All other images from Shutterstock.

Teacher Created Materials

5301 Oceanus Drive
Huntington Beach, CA 92649-1030
http://www.tcmpub.com
ISBN 978-1-4333-4826-6

Table of Contents

Everyone Is an Artist

In preschool, children love to paint. No one cares if the pictures are perfect. Children draw pictures to share their feelings. And older artists remember these feelings when they make art.

Many artists begin the day in art class. The students sit around a **model** to practice sketching. Drawing **portraits** is an ancient art. When the weather is nice, the class goes outside. This is the perfect place to draw **landscapes** from nature.

"Every child is an artist. The problem is how to remain an artist once he grows up."

—Pablo Picasso

THINK LINK

Imagine you are an artist.
- ➤ What skills would you need to succeed?
- ➤ How does someone earn money as an artist?
- ➤ What type of artist would you like to be?

An Artist's Day

An artist's day may look something like this.

7:30	A.M.	Wake up, dress comfortably.
8:00	A.M.	Eat breakfast and walk to art class.
9:00	A.M.	Sketch in art class.
12:00	P.M.	Break for lunch with other art students.
12:30	P.M.	Take brisk walk to the **studio**.
1:00	P.M.	Prepare the **canvas**. Set up the **easel**, **palette**, paints, and brushes.
1:15	P.M.	Begin painting.
3:00	P.M.	Take a 15-minute stretch break, then keep painting.
5:00	P.M.	Clean the brushes and palette. The painting will be finished tomorrow.
5:30	P.M.	Enjoy dinner.
6:30	P.M.	Shower and dress up for the fun evening ahead.
7:00	P.M.	Time for the **exhibit**.
10:00	P.M.	The exhibit ends.
11:00	P.M.	Sleep!

Experts say it takes 10,000 hours of practice to master an activity.

6

STOP! THINK...

- What are you usually doing at 9:00 in the morning?

- When do you feel the most creative?

- Why do you think artists say they never have enough time to make art?

Mighty Media

There are many kinds of artists. Some are painters. Others are **illustrators** or **sculptors**. Each type of art uses different tools. The supplies are called **media**. Art can be made from anything. It can be made from wire, cardboard, or even sand at the beach! What matters is that the art was made with care and imagination.

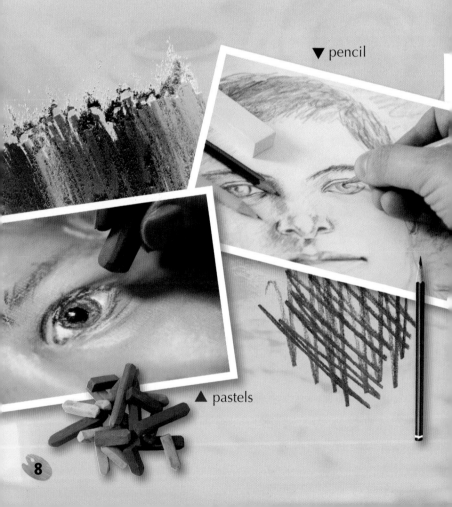

▼ pencil

▲ pastels

During class, artists talk about what media they would like to try. Some want to use pencils and pens to draw. Others may use crayons or **pastels** to add color. **Charcoal** can be used to make a strong dark line. Each tool creates a different effect. Some make thin sharp lines. Others add color and look softer. Artists like to try new tools and see what happens.

◀ paint

▼ ink

▼ charcoal

Other artists prefer to paint instead of draw. There are many kinds of paints. **Watercolors** are dry paints. Artists mix them with water to create washes of color. They are usually painted with soft brushes on paper. **Acrylics** are painted on canvas with firmer brushes. They can also be painted on wood with a small knife. It's just like frosting a cake! Acrylics are popular because they can be used in so many different ways. **Oil paints** are thick. **Linseed oil** is often mixed in to thin them. They take a much longer time to dry than other paints. They are painted in layers. And every layer needs time to dry.

Sculptures can be tiny or huge. They can be made from almost anything. The most popular sculpting materials are clay, bronze, and marble. Fabric, glass, and wood have also been used. These are just some of the media artists use to make art. And new ways of using media are always being tested.

◄ The terracotta warriors are more than 2,000 years old. These ancient Chinese sculptures are made of clay.

◀ Marcel Duchamp's
Bicycle Wheel

Oddities in Art

Art can be made from anything. Marcel Duchamp attached a bicycle wheel to a kitchen stool and called it art. Other artists have used candy, butter, leaves, and even human hair to make art!

Not-So-Trashy Art

One person's trash can be an artist's treasure. That is why many artists make art using recycled materials. They use cardboard, metal, plastic, pieces of cloth, and leather. Artists make paintings, jewelry, sculptures, toys, and furniture.

Many people like to make art using "trash." There is a recycled art program near Los Angeles, California. Trucks filled with clean recycled supplies pull up to the school. Inside, kids can find odds and ends such as scraps of leather, bottle caps, and glittery paper to use in their art projects.

Can you imagine the art that can be made from old bicycles? That is what two artists used to build this 65-foot-tall sculpture.

Robert Bradford's *Foo Foo 2*, was made from thousands of old toys.

Can you tell what was used to create this monster? ▶

Imagine That

Before the brush hits the canvas, artists must think about what to paint. Artists make quick sketches to plan their work. A sketch is a rough drawing. This helps artists try different ideas before deciding on their final idea. They might paint a portrait or it may be a landscape. Sometimes artists use images from their minds.

Artists may paint for themselves. But they can paint for others, too. When an artist is hired to paint a picture, it is a **commission**. Other paintings may be sold in art galleries. But not all pieces are for sale. Artists make many paintings for fun. Others are made for practice. These daily activities help artists develop their skills.

What Inspires You?

Do you ever see or hear something that makes you feel great? Does this feeling make you want to dance or sing or even draw a picture? Artists can be inspired when they hear a song or see a sunset. What inspires you?

On Location

Some artists like working in a studio at home. This is a quiet easy place to work. Others, especially landscape painters, like to work outside. This is sometimes called working **en plein air** (ahn ple NER). This French phrase means "in the open air."

Artists rest a blank canvas on an easel. The first step is to sketch an idea on the canvas. Next the palette is prepared. A rainbow of paints is squeezed on the palette. With these paints, artists can mix more colors right on the palette.

Some artists draw chalk art on the sidewalks in busy cities. Others paint murals on the walls of public buildings.

En Plein Air

The **Impressionists** of the 1870s made working outside popular. They loved to capture the beauty of sunsets, fog, and other natural wonders.

The Artist's Toolbox

Artists use a wide variety of supplies to create their work.

Blending stumps are used to blend lines and colors together. Some artists use them to shade a pencil drawing. They come in various thicknesses and lengths. The paper can be removed or sanded off so it is clean.

A putty eraser is gentler on paper than a hard eraser. It is less likely to damage the paper. Some artists dab small areas. Others erase in streaks.

Pencils range from hard to soft. A label at the top shows how hard or soft it is. The labels include a number and a letter.

A palette is a board painters use to mix colors. Some artists stand at their easel holding the palette in one hand and a paintbrush in the other.

A canvas is made of cotton or linen stretched over a wooden frame. Artists used wooden panels before they began using canvas.

Paintbrushes come in many different sizes. Oil and acrylic brushes have long handles. Watercolor paintbrushes have shorter handles.

Meet Roy G. Biv

Many artists put the paints on the palette in a special order. It's in the same order that colors are seen in a rainbow. A great way to remember these colors is by thinking of Roy G. Biv. This isn't the name of a real person. Look at the first letters of the words *red*, *orange*, *yellow*, *green*, *blue*, *indigo*, and *violet*. They make up Roy G. Biv.

Paint tubes come in many colors. Mixing colors creates new colors. Red, yellow, and blue are primary colors. These colors are used to make orange, green, and violet. Artists add white to lighten colors. Adding a bit of black can make the colors darker.

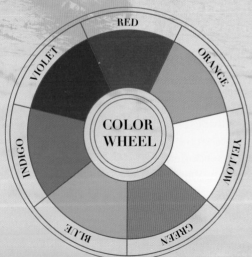

COLOR WHEEL

RED
ORANGE
YELLOW
GREEN
BLUE
INDIGO
VIOLET

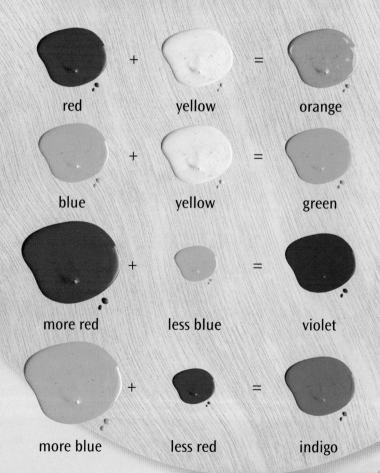

Rainbow Math

Try your own rainbow math project. See how many colors you can create with some paint, brushes, and new color palettes. Don't forget your new friend Roy G. Biv!

red + yellow = orange

blue + yellow = green

more red + less blue = violet

more blue + less red = indigo

Every Picture Tells a Story

Many artists are inspired by two famous paintings. One is *Starry Night*. It was painted by Vincent van Gogh (van GAW) around 1889. This picture shows the night sky as van Gogh imagined it from his bedroom window. It was painted in a special **style**. **Post-Impressionism** is a very personal style of painting. These artists use light and color to share their feelings.

At moments when it doesn't feel like there is enough time to paint, artists may remember another painting: *The Persistence of Memory*. This is a painting of melting clocks. It was painted around 1931 by Salvador Dalí. This dreamy style is known as **Surrealism**.

Star Bright

"This morning I saw the country from my window a long time before sunrise," van Gogh wrote to his brother, "with nothing but the morning star, which looked very big." The "morning star" he mentioned was the planet Venus. Those famous words may describe van Gogh's **inspiration** for the stars in his famous painting *Starry Night*.

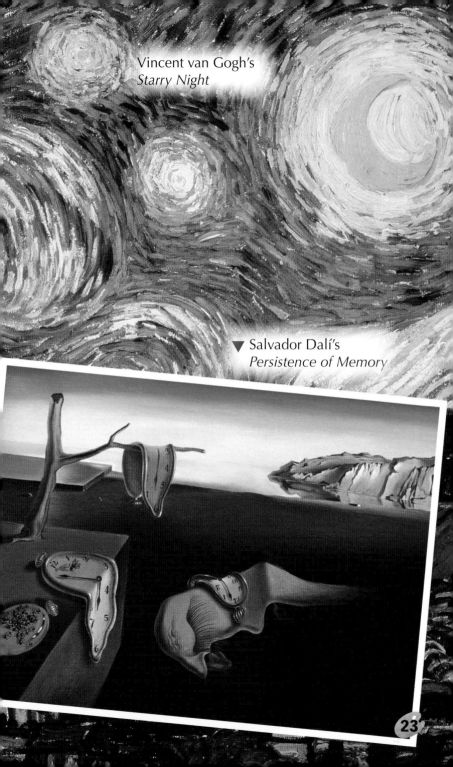

Vincent van Gogh's
Starry Night

▼ Salvador Dalí's
Persistence of Memory

The Latest Style

Styles change in art just as they do in fashion. Art history includes many styles. These changing styles are called *art movements*. Knowing when and where a painting was made is important. These facts help us know why it was made. They help us understand what story an artist wanted to tell. **Expressionism** is a style many artists use to tell a story. This style lets artists show their strong feelings about life.

Expressionism

Cubism

Realism

Painting Lives!

Every few years, people declare that painting is "dead." This means they think there is nothing new to paint. They believe every style of painting has already been created. But this never ends up being true. After a few years, painting always becomes popular again.

Impressionism

Surrealism

DIG DEEPER!

This *Ism,* That *Ism*

Art history includes a wide variety of movements. This time line begins with cave art, an early form of art. There are so many styles to choose from to paint this dog!

Cave Art
(over 30,000 years ago)
People from prehistoric times used torch soot and paint made from plants. ▶

▲ Pop Art
(1950s)
These artists looked at common objects and people in new ways.

Surrealism
(1920s–1940s)
This art did not show the real world. It included imaginary creatures or objects that looked unreal.

Renaissance
(1300–1602)
Artists wanted their work to be balanced and calm.

Impressionism
(1863–1890)
These artists took their canvases outside to use natural light to create colorful paintings. ▶

▲ Cubism
(1907–1914)
Objects and people were shown from more than one point of view.

▲ Expressionism
(1905–1930)
This art used strange shapes, colors, and lines to show feelings instead of reality.

Magic Time

"Imagination is more important than knowledge."

—Albert Einstein

This is one of the most famous quotes of all time. Many artists take classes to learn new **techniques** (tek-NEEKS). But there is more to being an artist than technical skills. There is the magic of imagination.

When an artist paints, it is a magical time. It is a time when skills and creativity come together to make something new. While painting, the artist forgets about time. The artist enters the world of imagination.

Making art may not always be easy. But it is always a special time. Painters, dancers, and singers are all artists who enjoy this special time.

The Arts Take Smarts

There are many ways to be creative. Painting, drawing, sculpture, music, dance, and theater are all known as *the arts*. Artists study very hard to become good at what they love to do.

Edgar Degas's *The Little Fourteen-Year-Old Dancer* ▶

Inspiration

Artists are always looking for inspiration. Some find it by being in nature. Most artists like to spend time with other artists, including writers and actors. They give one another ideas.

Arty Party

When an exhibit opens, there is a **reception**. This is a fun party! It is where artists can share their art. There may be food, music, and drinks. Artists usually invite family and friends to these parties. Receptions are a fun way for artists to make new friends, too.

Original art has something special. It makes people want to see it up close. Sometimes, people like paintings so much they want to buy them. Paintings can be sold at receptions. Most artists have exhibits so they can sell art. It takes many people working together for a show to go well. Artists are thankful for the help of others.

The First Exhibits?

The first known paintings were created nearly 30,000 years ago on the walls of dark caves. It's fun to imagine that cave paintings were the first art exhibits ever!

Show Time!

After long days of drawing and painting, it's time for an exhibit. It's show time! After working alone all day, artists are excited to spend time with friends and family.

An exhibit, or show, is a special event. Art is hung on walls. It may be lit with spotlights. An exhibit can be at a **gallery** or **museum.** Or it might be at a library, a school, or another meeting place. Some exhibits display and sell art for a short time. Other art pieces are not for sale. These may be shown in **permanent** places, like museums.

Art students love to check out exhibits so they can get ideas for their own work.

A reporter from the local newspaper has come to review the artwork. Tomorrow there will be a story about the exhibit.

Artists invite friends and family to attend the exhibit.

The gallery owner is looking for visitors who may like to buy a piece of art.

This looks like a potential buyer. What price will he offer for the painting?

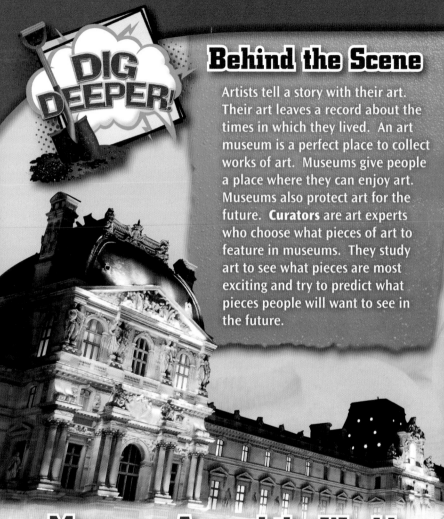

DIG DEEPER!

Behind the Scene

Artists tell a story with their art. Their art leaves a record about the times in which they lived. An art museum is a perfect place to collect works of art. Museums give people a place where they can enjoy art. Museums also protect art for the future. **Curators** are art experts who choose what pieces of art to feature in museums. They study art to see what pieces are most exciting and try to predict what pieces people will want to see in the future.

Museums Around the World

▼ Smithsonian Museum of Art, Washington, DC

▼ Metropolitan Museum of Art, New York, NY

▼ The Vatican Museums, Rome, Italy

One of the most well-known museums throughout the world is the Louvre (LOO-vruh) in Paris, France. This museum has a very famous painting that people come from all over the world to see. Have you heard of the *Mona Lisa*?

▲ Leonardo da Vinci's *Mona Lisa*

▼ Getty Museum, Los Angeles, CA

▼ Guggenheim Museum, Bilbao, Spain

▼ National Gallery, London, England

An Attitude of Gratitude

When an artist sells a piece, it is an exciting day! The family who bought the painting will take it home. They will add it to their art collection. The artist is paid for the work. Some of this money goes to the gallery owner. Galleries need money to pay for art exhibits and receptions. Some artists must pay their **agents**, too. Agents get paid to help artists with the business of selling art. Artists are grateful for the help of agents and galleries.

Counting Pennies

Most artists don't make enough money selling their artwork in galleries. They must take on other art jobs. Here are some of the other ways artists can make money.

▲ Create art for calendars or notecards.

Display artwork for sale at an art fair.

▲ Teach art classes.

◀ Illustrate books and magazines.

Sell art to businesses to use with their products.

Starry Night

Exhibits are exciting. But the real magic of being an artist is making art. It is messy. It takes time. And artists never know where the next idea will come from. Artists find inspiration everywhere, even in the night sky. Walking back from an exhibit may be the perfect time to plan a new project— especially on a starry night.

▲ Vincent van Gogh's, *Self Portrait*

What's Your Style?

Just as no one is exactly like someone else, no art style is exactly alike. The art you like best is the art that will inspire you. Paint a picture in your favorite style and have an art exhibit with your friends. You may learn something new about your friends...and about yourself!

Interview with an Artist

Rosi Sanchez was born in Spain, where she studied art and theater. She moved to the United States when she was 21 and opened Rosita's World of Arts and Crafts in Huntington Beach, California. There, she sold her artwork and the work of other artists for several years. She is now retired, enjoys her grandchildren, and continues to exhibit her art in Laguna Beach.

Michael: Hello Rosi! When did you first become an artist?

Rosi: I made my first painting when I was nine years old. I only had two tubes of paint: brown and white. So I painted a white poodle against a brown wall. I had heard of oil painting, but I didn't know that it took special oils made just for painting. Not knowing this, I mixed my paints with olive oil used for cooking! My family thought this was funny. They loved my painting, and that's when I knew I wanted to be an artist.

Blanca: When was your first exhibit?

Rosi: I entered my first art exhibit when I was 13. It was a painting of two girls in kimonos in a Japanese flower garden. That show was a contest, and I won second prize! It was very exciting. I've sold and exhibited many art pieces since then.

Michael: Did you study art?

Rosi: Yes, I studied art at the Instituto Mengual in Madrid, Spain. I loved school. I feel that artists should also study after school on their own. Practicing every day is the best way to learn anything.

Blanca: Is there an artist you admire?

Rosi: Pablo Picasso. He dared to try new things, and he valued children as great artists.

Michael: What's best about being an artist?

Rosi: Looking forward to each day because I have a job doing what I love!

Key:
🎤 interviewers
🖌 artist

Madrid
●
SPAIN

41

Glossary

acrylics—a type of paint artists use

agents—people or businesses that act on another's behalf

canvas—a strong cloth used as a surface for painting

charcoal—compressed burned wood that can be used for drawing

commission—a special request for an artist to create specific artwork in exchange for payment

curators—the people in charge of a museum or art collection

easel—a stand for supporting a canvas

en plein air—a French expression meaning "in the open air"

exhibit—a public display of a collection of art pieces

Expressionism—the artistic style in which colors and images are distorted or exaggerated for expressive purposes

gallery—a building used to display or sell paintings or other art

illustrators—people who create drawings for books or magazines

Impressionists—artists who followed the art movement in 19th-century France that focused on light, color, movement, and nature

inspiration—something that moves the mind or the emotions

landscapes—pictures that show the view of an area or natural scenery

linseed oil—a drying oil

media—materials used in a work of art, such as paint, pencil, or clay

model—a person or thing that serves as the subject for an artist

museum—a building that displays important artistic, historic, or scientific objects

oil paints—type of paint made from colored powder and a special oil

palette—a board used by a painter to lay and mix pigments

pastels—a chalklike crayon

permanent—lasting forever

portraits—paintings or drawings, especially of a face, that looks like a certain person or pet

Post-Impressionism—a movement in art that used thick applications of paint, rich colors, distinctive brushstrokes, and distorted shapes

reception—a party or gathering where an artist can share his or her art

sculptors—artists that carve or mold different material into decorative three-dimensional objects or statues

studio—the room or space where an artist creates art

style—the way that a piece of art looks and how it tells something about when and where it was created

Surrealism—the art movement beginning in the 1920s that focused on dreams and symbolism

techniques—skills or crafts used by an artist to create a certain style or effect

watercolors—a type of paint used with water

Index

Bibliography

Kelen, Emery. Leonardo da Vinci's Advice to Artists. Running Press, 1990.

Leonardo Da Vinci's artwork accompanies some of his thoughts on color, landscapes, emotions and more. The information comes from his personal notebooks.

Kohl, MaryAnn F. and Solga, Kim. *Discovering Great Artists: Hands–On Art for Children in the Styles of the Great Masters.* **Bright Ring Publishing, 1997.**

Try your hand at a wide variety of art techniques. The activities are meant for artists of all ages.

Luxbacher, Irene. *The Jumbo Book of Art.* **Kids Can Press, 2003.**

This book teaches kids basic techniques for painting, drawing, sculpting, and more through step-by-step projects and activities.

Schwake, Susan. *Art Lab for Kids.* **Quarry Books, 2012**

This book includes 52 adventures in drawing, painting, and other media—a project for every week of the year!

Wenzel, Angela. *13 Artists Children Should Know.* **Prestel Pub, 2009.**

Learn about 13 of the most famous artists throughout history. This book tells about the artists, their lives, and their work. Games and activities are also included.

More to Explore

Most Famous Paintings of All Time

http://www.usefulcharts.com/history/most-famous-paintings-of-all-time.html

This website shows 25 of the most famous artists throughout history. They are listed based on when they lived and include an example of their artwork.

BRUSHster

http://www.nga.gov/kids/zone/brushster.htm

BRUSHster allows you to create colorful works of art on your computer screen. You can change the effects of the brush, the strokes, the colors, and more. Then, save your work of art or print it and share it with others.

The Art Project

http://www.googleartproject.com

Google's Art Project provides virtual tours of famous museums around the world, such as the Metropolitan Museum of Art in New York City. You can zoom in on individual pieces of art and even create your own art.

Art from Scrap

http://artfromscrap.org

Art from Scrap helps kids understand the importance of being creative and caring for the environment. They recycle thousands of pounds of clean materials and sell them to others to create art, costumes, and more.

National Gallery of Art

http://www.nga.gov/kids

The National Gallery of Art is a great place to visit when you're in Washington, DC. If you can't make it there, visit this site to explore the online galleries and make your own art.

About the Authors

Michael Serwich is a professional puppeteer and performer. He has a bachelor of fine arts (BFA) in playwriting from De Paul University. He writes and hosts puppet shows at The Natural History Museum of Los Angeles. His favorite puppet there is a life-sized juvenile T-Rex named Hunter.

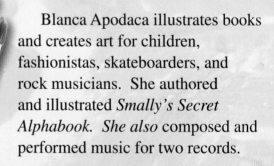

Blanca Apodaca illustrates books and creates art for children, fashionistas, skateboarders, and rock musicians. She authored and illustrated *Smally's Secret Alphabook. She also* composed and performed music for two records.

Together, Blanca and her husband Michael are artists who write stories and build puppet shows, but their greatest creation will always be their daughter, Melody.